GROUP ACTIVITIES TO INCLUDE STUDENTS WITH SPECIAL NEEDS

GROUP ACTIVITIES TO INCLUDE STUDENTS WITH SPECIAL NEEDS

Developing
Social
Interactive
Skills

JULIA WILKINS

CORWIN PRESS, INC.
A Sage Publications Company
Thousand Oaks, California

Copyright © 2001 by Corwin Press, Inc.

For information:

Corwin Press, Inc.
A Sage Publications Company
2455 Teller Road
Thousand Oaks, California 91320
E-mail: order@corwinpress.com

Sage Publications Ltd.
6 Bonhill Street
London EC2A 4PU
United Kingdom

Sage Publications India Pvt. Ltd.
M-32 Market
Greater Kailash I
New Delhi 110 048 India

Printed in the United States of America

Library of Congress Cataloging-in-Publication Data

Wilkins, Julia.
    Group activities to include students with special needs:
Developing social interactive skills / by Julia Wilkins.
        p.   cm.
    ISBN 0-7619-7725-2 (cloth: alk. paper)
    ISBN 0-7619-7726-0 (pbk.: alk. paper)
    1. Handicapped children—Education (Elementary).   2. Special
education—Activity programs.   3. Educational games.   4. Social
skills—Study and teaching (Elementary).   I. Title.
    LC4026.W54   2000
    371.9'043—dc21   00-008538

This book is printed on acid-free paper.

01   02   03   04   05   10   9   8   7   6   5   4   3   2   1

Corwin Editorial Assistant: Kylee Liegl
Production Editor: Denise Santoyo
Editorial Assistant: Victoria Cheng
Typesetter/Designer: Janelle LeMaster
Illustrations by: Jody Tassone

Contents

PART THREE: Ball Games 171

Preface

All students in special education programs have individualized education plans. As a consequence, lessons tend to be based on the specific needs of each student. The low teacher-to-student ratio in special education classes makes this possible and allows students to receive the one-on-one attention they need to attain their goals. The result is that individual student achievement often becomes the focus, leaving little time for group activities. Consequently, there is frequently little interaction between students who often already lack appropriate social skills.

Many students in special education programs have difficulty relating to others and interacting with peers. When interactions are negative, students are often prevented from working or playing together.

This book encourages teachers to help students develop the social skills they need to interact appropriately. Rather than discouraging students from playing together, it is recommended that group activities be incorporated into the daily routine. Activities have been designed so that they can be carried out without prior planning. Games can therefore be taken from this book any time the teacher feels students could benefit from positive interaction and teamwork.

Activities have been designed so that group members can take advantage of their combined physical and mental capabilities. "Winning" a game is not the goal—the purpose is to gain a sense of working together as a team. The games emphasize participation, cooperation, mutual support, and improvement of self-esteem. By participating in these activities, children develop basic skills while interacting with one another in supportive groups.

Choosing Appropriate Activities

This book is divided into three parts and contains more than 120 activities accompanied by easy to follow, step-by-step directions. Chapters are divided into classroom games, gym and outdoor games, and ball games. Activities should obviously be chosen based on the physical space available. Ball games should be conducted in a large area such as a gym or playground, and have been included as separate chapters for teachers needing to promote large motor movement and hand-eye coordination.

Within each chapter, activities are divided into Level 1 and Level 2 games. Games should be selected according to the ability levels of the students. The following descriptions of Level 1 and Level 2 games should help teachers choose appropriate activities.

Level 1

Level 1 games are suitable for students functioning at an early elementary grade level. They have been designed for students who are non-verbal and for those who can carry out one- and two-step directions with assistance. One-on-one assistance may be required at different levels of intensity and will be determined by the level of independence in the group.

Level 2

Level 2 games have been designed for students functioning at approximately a third-grade level and above. They are appropriate for students who have the ability to follow multiple-step directions and who are capable of following directions with minimal assistance. Many activities address verbal, communication, and pre-academic skills.

An index is provided at each level indicating the areas of skill development addressed by the activities. These include fine and large motor skills, hand-eye coordination, auditory processing, visual perception, following directions, and academic skills. This is followed by a list of these skills and the activities that can be used for developing them. This list should be used by teachers who wish to target particular areas of weakness.

On activity pages, the equipment needed and appropriate locations for carrying out the games are given. Skills developed through the activities and the abilities needed to participate are also provided. Some activities require sight, hearing, or speech. These and any other abilities necessary to partake effectively in the games are indicated through the use of icons.

A key for icons is given below:

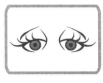 Sight

 Hearing

 Speech

 Leg Ambulation

 Arm Ambulation

 Academic (basic adding, reading/writing)

 All Students (no restrictions)

Visually Impaired and Blind Students

If there are students who are visually impaired or blind in the group, it is recommended that teachers acquire the following equipment:

1. *Portable sound sources that can be set to play different sounds at varied pitches and speeds.* These can be used to help direct students and are particularly useful when activities involve running to particular locations.

2. *Beepers.* These can be inserted into bean bags or attached to objects such as basketball nets.

3. *Balls with internal sound sources.* There are a variety of balls that make jingling or rattling sounds when thrown.

4. *Sound-makers for students.* Bells on bracelets that fasten with Velcro are recommended. These should be used to assist students with visual impairments to locate other students as they move around the play area.

5. *Fluorescent or brightly colored ink or tape.* These can be used to brighten various objects used in the activities.

Acknowledgments

I would like to thank Zeina Williams, teacher of the visually impaired, for her helpful suggestions, and Jody Tassone, who created the illustrations for this book. I would also like to thank the peer reviewers and Robb Clouse of Corwin Press.

In addition, the contributions of the following reviewers are gratefully acknowledged:

Merle Burbridge
Resource Specialist, Ramona Elementary School
Hemet Unified School District, Hemet, CA

Helen P. Johnston
Special Education Teacher, Calvert County Public Schools
Prince Frederick, MD

Karen Smith
Teacher, Saddle Brook Middle School
Saddle Brook, NJ

Rose M. Ray
Clinical Assistant Professor, Boston University
Boston, MA

Lori M. Ellis
Elementary Program Specialist, Alamogordo Public Schools,
    Department of Special Education
Alamogordo, NM

Kathleen McAnnich
Early Childhood Special Educator, Culpeper County Schools
Culpeper, VA

Lynn R. Zubov
Coordinator of Special Education Program, Department of Teacher
  Education
Canisius College, Buffalo, NY

About the Author

Julia Wilkins has written numerous journal articles and is coauthor of two books, *Math Activities for Young Children* and *Non-Competitive Motor Activities: A Guide for Elementary Classroom Teachers.* She is a special education teacher in the Buffalo Public Schools and an adjunct instructor of education at D'Youville College. She holds two master's degrees and is currently pursuing her doctorate in educational psychology at the University of Buffalo.

PART ONE

Classroom Games

1

Classroom Games

Level 1 Activities

Level 1 Classroom Games

Level 1 Classroom Games—by Skills

Following Directions

Visual Perception

Verbal Communication

Creative Thinking

Beanbag Bridges

Equipment:	• Beanbags
	• 12-inch rulers
Locations:	• Classroom, gymnasium, outdoors
Skill Development:	Fine motor, large motor, hand-eye coordination, following directions, visual perception

Abilities Required: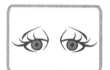

Activity: Children stand in pairs, each with one ruler and one beanbag. Each child holds one end of the ruler and the beanbag is placed in the middle. Children then begin to move around the room with the beanbag balanced on the ruler. The teacher gives directions as to how to walk, such as crouching down, or with arms raised above their heads. These actions should be demonstrated for children who are hearing impaired.

Figure 1.1. Beanbag Bridges

Additional Notes:

_____

_____

_____

_____

_____

_____

_____

_____

_____

_____

_____

_____

_____

_____

_____

_____

_____

_____

_____

_____

_____

_____

_____

_____

_____

_____

_____

_____

_____

_____

_____

_____

_____

_____

_____

Create a Maze

Equipment:	• Ball of string
Location:	• Classroom, gymnasium, outdoors
Skill Development:	Fine motor, hand-eye coordination, visual perception

Abilities Required:

Activity: Children stand in circle formation. One child has a ball of string and begins the game by holding onto the end of the string with one hand and throwing the ball to someone else in the circle with the other hand. That child takes hold of the string and throws the ball to someone else in the circle. When the last child receives the ball of string, the children continue throwing in reverse order, with each child throwing the ball back to the person they received it from. Each child rewinds her string back onto the ball before throwing it on to the next child. The last child to receive the ball of string should be the child who began the game.

Figure 1.2. Create a Maze

Additional Notes:

Dog and Bone

Equipment:	• Cut-out bone
	• Sticky tack
Location:	• Classroom
Skill Development:	Large motor, auditory processing, verbal communication

Abilities Required:

Activity: One child is the "dog" and sits on a chair in front of the other children with his back to them. A cut-out bone is stuck to the back of the chair with a piece of sticky tack. The children line up on the other side of the room. The first child in line creeps up behind the dog and tries to steal the bone from the back of the chair. If the dog hears the child, he turns around and says, "Leave my bone alone," at which point the child returns to the end of the line. The next player then tries to steal the bone. The first child to reach the bone without being detected changes places with the dog. If the dog wrongly accuses someone of trying to steal his bone, he goes to the end of the line and the next child in line becomes the dog. Children who are non-verbal can ring a bell or sound a buzzer when they hear a bone thief approaching. Children who are blind should be paired with sighted partners.

Additional Notes:

_____

_____

_____

_____

_____

_____

_____

_____

_____

_____

Color Hunters

Equipment: • Colored material

Location: • Classroom, gymnasium, outdoors

Skill Development: Large motor, following directions, auditory processing,
                        visual perception

Abilities Required:

Activity: Children are seated in circle formation, except one child who is the "color
                        hunter" and stands in the middle. The teacher calls out a color and the
                        color hunter looks for the color on the children's clothes. If he finds the
                        color on any item of clothing, he approaches the child and points to the
                        color. The seated child and child in the middle then switch positions. For
                        children who are hearing impaired, the teacher should hold up a col-
                        ored piece of material to indicate the color to be found on the children's
                        clothing.

Additional Notes: _____

                        _____

                        _____

                        _____

                        _____

                        _____

                        _____

                        _____

                        _____

                        _____

                        _____

                        _____

                        _____

                        _____

                        _____

Footprints

Equipment:	• Construction paper • Markers • Scissors • Masking tape • Music source
Location:	• Classroom, gymnasium
Skill Development:	Large motor, visual perception, auditory processing
Abilities Required:	

Activity: Children trace around their feet on two pieces of construction paper, with each foot on a different sheet. The footprints are then taped around the room at such a distance that children can easily step on them without having to touch the floor. Children stand in a row holding hands and the first child in line leads the group around the room to the rhythm of the music. Children step from footprint to footprint. When the music is paused, children stop in their tracks and check that they are standing on a footprint. Children who are blind should be placed next to a sighted guide.

Figure 1.3. Footprints

Additional Notes:
_____
_____
_____
_____
_____
_____
_____
_____
_____
_____
_____
_____
_____
_____
_____
_____
_____
_____
_____
_____
_____
_____
_____
_____
_____
_____
_____
_____
_____
_____
_____
_____
_____
_____

It's Not a Scarf!

Equipment: • Scarf

Location: • Classroom

Skill Development: Fine motor, auditory processing, visual perception, creative thinking

Abilities Required: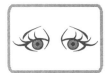

Activity: Children sit on chairs in circle formation. The teacher holds a scarf and begins the game by wrapping the scarf around her wrist to demonstrate that it is not really a scarf, but a bracelet. When the children guess that it is being used as a bracelet, the teacher hands it to someone else in the group who thinks of another use. The child may wrap the scarf around her head indicating that it is a head wrap. When the children correctly guess that it is a head wrap, the scarf is passed to the next player in the circle. Children wait for someone to guess correctly how they are using the scarf before passing it on.

Figure 1.4. It's Not a Scarf!

Additional Notes:

Quiet Ball

Equipment:	• Large, soft, ball/beeper ball
Location:	• Classroom
Skill Development:	Hand-eye coordination, visual perception
Abilities Required:	
Activity:	Children stand by their desks. One child has a ball and starts the game by throwing it to another child in the group. The object of the game is for children to throw the ball and catch it without moving away from their desks, and without making any noise. Each player throws the ball immediately so that the ball moves quickly and silently around the room. A beeper ball can be used for children who are blind and the child's name should be said out loud as the ball is being thrown. For children who are visually impaired, a brightly colored ball should be used. Balls decorated with stripes made from black electrical tape can also be effective for children with visual impairments.

Figure 1.5. Quiet Ball

Additional Notes:

Tangles

Equipment:	• None
Location:	• Classroom, gymnasium, outdoors
Skill Development:	Fine motor, large motor
Abilities Required:	
Activity:	Children are divided into groups of five or six, and stand in circle formation. Each child joins hands with the person standing next to him or her in the group. Everyone's right hand should be joined with another child's left and vice versa. When the whole group is holding hands, children try to untangle themselves without letting go of each other's hand grips. Children in wheelchairs should be positioned next to standing children.

Figure 1.6. Tangles

Additional Notes:

Where's My Partner?

Equipment: • None

Location: • Classroom, gymnasium, outdoors

Skill Development: Large motor, visual/spatial perception

Abilities Required:

Activity: Children stand in pairs holding hands, an arm's length apart. With their eyes closed, they drop each other's hands and turn around in place three times. Then, without opening their eyes, they try to relocate their partners by stretching out their arms and finding each other's hands again. When they are back in their original position, they open their eyes and shake hands with their partners. Children in wheelchairs should move their chairs away from their partner and turn around at least once before trying to relocate their partner.

Figure 1.7. Where's My Partner?

Additional Notes:

Who's Missing?

Equipment:	• None
Location:	• Classroom
Skill Development:	Visual perception, auditory processing, verbal communication
Abilities Required:	

Activity: Children sit randomly behind their desks or in circle formation. One child is selected to be the "guesser" and leaves the room. A child from inside the class hides somewhere, such as behind a bookshelf or door. When the guesser returns, he has to guess who the missing person is. After three guesses, the hiding child can give a clue by speaking. If the guesser is blind, children should state their names before the guesser leaves the room. When he returns, children who are not hiding should take turns saying, "I'm here." The child will guess who is missing by process of elimination.

Figure 1.8. Who's Missing?

Additional Notes:

Do This, Do That

Equipment: • None

Location: • Classroom, gymnasium

Skill Development: Large motor, auditory processing, following directions

Abilities Required:

Activity: Children sit behind their desks or in circle formation in the gym. The teacher asks the children to respond to the following directions while paying attention to other children in the group who respond in the same way. The directions should be as follows: "If you have a brother, clap your hands. If you have a sister, raise your hand. If you have a pet, stamp your feet. If you like school, wave your arms. If you like playing outside, jump up. If you like watching movies, nod your head. If you like riding your bike, raise your right hand. If you like sleeping, raise your left hand." At the end of the game children should be asked who in the class they have things in common with. If students have limited physical mobility, directions should be adapted accordingly.

Additional Notes: _____

                       _____

                       _____

                       _____

                       _____

                       _____

                       _____

                       _____

                       _____

                       _____

                       _____

                       _____

Touch Something

Equipment:	• None
Location:	• Classroom, outdoors
Skill Development:	Large motor, auditory processing, following directions, visual perception

Abilities Required:

Activity: This game should be carried out in a large open area. The object of the game is for children to touch something as directed by the teacher before she counts to 10. The teacher begins by making commands such as, "Touch something hard," "Touch something blue," and "Touch something small." The children run around the room trying to touch an appropriate object before the teacher counts to 10. When the teacher reaches 10, she calls, "Time's up!" and then gives another command. Students can also be given the opportunity to call out commands.

Additional Notes: _____

_____

_____

_____

_____

_____

_____

_____

_____

_____

_____

_____

_____

_____

_____

_____

Find the Color

Equipment:	• None
Location:	• Classroom
Skill Development:	Large motor, visual perception, auditory processing, following directions

Abilities Required:

Activity: Students are seated in circle formation, with a break in the middle, dividing them into two groups. The teacher directs children from one group to get up and touch something blue on the students on the other side of the circle and then return to their seats. When all the children are reseated, the roles are reversed, with children being told to touch something black on children in the other group. The game continues in this fashion with the teacher giving directions for children to touch different things on children sitting on the other side of the circle. For children who are hearing impaired, objects or signs displaying the colors to be found should be used.

Additional Notes: _____
_____
_____
_____
_____
_____
_____
_____
_____
_____
_____
_____

Listen to Me!

Equipment:	• None
Location:	• Classroom, gymnasium
Skill Development:	Large motor, auditory processing, following directions
Abilities Required:	
Activity:	Children sit behind their desks or in circle formation in the gym. They are instructed to listen carefully to the teacher's commands and to follow her directions accordingly. The directions should begin as follows: "Everyone, please stand," and then continue with: "Everyone wearing blue, please sit. If you are wearing sneakers, clap once. Everyone with brown hair, please stand. Everyone with blue eyes, please wave. Everyone wearing red, please sit. Everyone with blond hair, please shake your hands in the air. Everyone who is happy, please jump up once. Everyone who is wearing jeans, please sit." The game continues in this fashion with the teacher speeding up the instructions as the game goes along. For children who are blind, directions should be based on existing knowledge. Instructions should be adapted accordingly for students in wheelchairs.

Additional Notes:
_____
_____
_____
_____
_____
_____
_____
_____
_____
_____
_____
_____
_____

2

Classroom Games

Level 2 Activities

Level 2 Classroom Games

Level 2 Classroom Games—by Skills

Following Directions

Visual Perception

Verbal Communication

Academic

Creative Thinking

Adding Relay

Equipment:	• Chalkboard
	• Chalk
Location:	• Classroom
Skill Development:	Fine motor, large motor, academic, visual perception
Abilities Required:	  

Activity: Children are divided into two teams and line up in single file facing the chalkboard. The first player in each team runs up to the chalkboard and writes a two-digit number. The child then runs back to the group and hands the chalk to the second player in line. This child then runs to the chalkboard and writes a two-digit number directly under the first number. The game continues with each member of the group writing a different two-digit number under the previous one. The last player in the group adds all the numbers in her team's row. The game should be repeated so that all players have the chance to be the adder. The use of a dry erase board, which can be brought closer to students, may be more convenient for children in wheelchairs.

Figure 2.1. Adding Relay

Additional Notes:

Compliment Bags

Equipment:	• Brown paper bags
	• Pens
	• Paper
	• Thumb tacks
Location:	• Classroom
Skill Development:	Fine motor, academic, creative thinking, verbal communication
Abilities Required:	

Activity: Each child writes her name on the outside of a brown paper bag and pins the bag up somewhere in the room. Children then write positive messages to each child in the class and place them in the bags. The teacher should begin by brainstorming possible messages and then monitor what children write before the messages are placed in the bags. This activity can be extended over a period of time, with children writing messages each day and then reading them at the end of the week. Children who are unable to write should dictate their messages.

Figure 2.2. Compliment Bags

Additional Notes:

Fact or Fiction?

Equipment:	• None
Location:	• Classroom
Skill Development:	Verbal communication, auditory processing, creative thinking
Abilities Required:	

Activity: Children sit behind their desks in circle formation. The first child begins the game by telling the group two facts about himself—one fact and one fiction. For example, he may say something like, "I have two brothers" and, "I have been to Hawaii." The other children guess which is the true and which is the false statement. Children should have the chance to air their opinions one at a time. When every child has guessed, the group should take a vote on which statement was fact and which was fiction. The game continues in this way, with each child having the opportunity to say two things about himself. Statements should be written if there are children who are deaf or non-verbal in the group.

Additional Notes: _____

_____

_____

_____

_____

_____

_____

_____

_____

_____

_____

_____

_____

_____

Sometimes I'm Tall

Equipment:	• None
Location:	• Classroom, gymnasium, outdoors
Skill Development:	Large motor, auditory processing, following directions, verbal communication
Abilities Required:	

Activity: Children stand in circle formation, except for one child who is "It" and stands in the middle, blindfolded. When the teacher indicates with her hands, children in the circle stand on tiptoes and stretch their arms up while saying, "I'm very, very tall." When the teacher indicates the opposite action children crouch down toward the floor while saying, "I'm very, very small." They then alternate between, "Sometimes I'm tall," and "Sometimes I'm small." The actions are repeated a few times without the words, with children following the lead of the teacher's hand movements. The children then ask, "Guess what we are now?" The child in the middle tries to guess from the voices whether the group is tall or small.

Additional Notes: _____
_____
_____
_____
_____
_____
_____
_____
_____
_____
_____
_____
_____
_____

Find the Leader

Equipment:	• None
Location:	• Classroom, gymnasium
Skill Development:	Large motor, following directions, visual perception
Abilities Required:	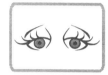

Activity:

One child is the "guesser" and leaves the room while the other children stand in circle formation and follow the movements of a leader. When the guesser enters the room, she watches the movements of the children in the circle and tries to work out who the leader is. The leader may do things such as put his hand on his head or hop on one foot. The other children follow the actions, while trying not to look directly at the leader. The guesser has three chances to work out who the leader is. If the guesser is visually impaired, each child should have a different sound-maker, which she jingles or shakes as she is performing the actions. The guesser will work out who the leader is by the sound she hears first. The leader should adapt actions accordingly for children in wheelchairs.

Figure 2.3. Find the Leader

Additional Notes:

Buzz

Equipment: • None

Location: • Classroom

Skill Development: Verbal communication, auditory processing, academic

Abilities Required:

Activity: Children sit in circle formation at their desks. The object of the game is to substitute the word *buzz* for the word *four*. The players begin by counting off one number at a time, starting with one. The children say the correct number until it is time to say "Four," at which point the child says, "Buzz." Every time a four is in the number, the child says "Buzz" instead, so 14 is "Buzzteen," 34 is "Thirty-buzz," and 44 is "Buzz-ty-buzz." This game can be played with any number as the buzz number. For children who are non-verbal, the teacher walks around the outside of the circle and taps children on the shoulder while saying the numbers out loud. Children should stand up or raise their hands when the teacher says the buzz number.

Additional Notes: _____
                       _____
                       _____
                       _____
                       _____
                       _____
                       _____
                       _____
                       _____
                       _____
                       _____
                       _____
                       _____

Remember That, Copy Cat

Equipment:	• None
Location:	• Classroom, gymnasium, outdoors
Skill Development:	Large motor, following directions, visual perception, creative thinking
Abilities Required:	

Activity: Children stand in circle formation. One child begins the game by performing an action, such as touching his toes. The child next to him then repeats this action and adds another, such as twisting at the waist. The next child in line touches his toes, twists at the waist, and adds another action, such as a jumping jack. The game continues in this way, with children repeating the actions of others in correct sequence and adding an action of their own. For children who are visually impaired, the actions should be said out loud as children are performing them.

Additional Notes: _____

_____

_____

_____

_____

_____

_____

_____

_____

_____

_____

_____

_____

_____

_____

_____

Fox and Hound

Equipment:	• Small ball
	• Beanbag
Location:	• Classroom, gymnasium, outdoors
Skill Development:	Fine motor, hand-eye coordination, visual perception
Abilities Required:	 

Activity: Children stand in circle formation. A child on one side of the circle has a ball, which is the hound, and a child on the other side has a beanbag, which is the fox. The object of the game is for the hound to catch the fox. Both objects are passed around the circle, the aim being for the ball to end up in the same hands as the beanbag. Children pass the ball as quickly as they can around the circle so that it catches up with the beanbag. Children can change the direction in which the ball is being passed at any time to catch the beanbag coming from the opposite direction.

Figure 2.4. Fox and Hound

Additional Notes:

_____

_____

_____

_____

_____

_____

_____

_____

_____

_____

_____

_____

_____

_____

_____

_____

_____

_____

_____

_____

_____

_____

_____

_____

_____

_____

_____

_____

_____

_____

_____

_____

_____

_____

_____

_____

Grab Bag

Equipment:	• Toy car, airplane, rubber snake
	• Bag
	• Music
Location:	• Classroom, gymnasium
Skill Development:	Fine motor, large motor, following directions, visual perception, creative thinking

Abilities Required:

Activity: Children stand in circle formation and pass around a grab bag as the music plays. When the music stops, the child with the grab bag pulls an object from it and leads the children in moving like the object until the music resumes. For example, if an airplane is pulled from the bag, children should spread out their arms and pretend to be planes. Children may leave their seats and move creatively around the room. When the music resumes, children return to their seats and continue passing the grab bag around the circle. For students who are visually impaired, children should state what the object is as they remove it from the bag.

Figure 2.5. Grab Bag

Additional Notes:

I've Been There

Equipment:
- World map or U.S. map
- Thumb tacks

Location:
- Classroom

Skill Development: Fine motor, academic, verbal communication, auditory processing, creative thinking

Abilities Required:

Activity: A big map is displayed on the wall. Each child takes a turn placing a tack on the map to show somewhere else they have lived or visited. Children then pair up and talk to their partners about what it was like in that city or country. To help children find appropriate topics, the teacher may want to begin with a brainstorming session on aspects of life that may be different in other cities or countries and list these on the chalkboard. Children may want to discuss differences in the weather, food, places of interest, and recreational activities. Children then report back to the class, telling them about the city or country their partner visited and what life was like there.

Additional Notes: _____

_____

_____

_____

_____

_____

_____

_____

_____

_____

_____

_____

The Name Game

Equipment:	• None
Location:	• Classroom
Skill Development:	Verbal communication, auditory processing, creative thinking
Abilities Required:	

Activity: This activity is most effective if carried out on the first day of school, or used as an icebreaker. Children are seated on chairs in circle formation. One child begins the game by shaking hands with the student on his right, and introducing himself by saying his first name and another word that begins with the same letter as his first name, such as, "Hi, I'm Tom Turkey." The child then replies, "Hi Tom Turkey. My name is Ramon Rock." Ramon Rock then turns to the child on the other side of him and introduces himself. Children can also state one thing about themselves after stating their names, such as, "I like to listen to music." Students who are non-verbal can write their names or draw pictures and show them to the children sitting next to them.

Additional Notes: _____

_____

_____

_____

_____

_____

_____

_____

_____

_____

_____

_____

_____

Group Picture

Equipment:	• Large pieces of paper
	• Crayons or colored pencils
Location:	• Classroom
Skill Development:	Fine motor, following directions, visual perception, creative thinking

Abilities Required: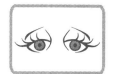

Activity: Students sit at their desks in groups of three. The first child in each group has a large piece of paper and follows the directions of the teacher as she describes a strange looking creature to be drawn. This child draws the head, which may be described as follows, "This creature has a big hairy head with horns and one large eye." When the head is complete, the student passes the picture to the child next to him who draws the body from the neck to the waist. The creature may have a fat belly, long dangly arms with eight fingers, or maybe even wings. The last child draws the legs, feet, and toes. When the picture is complete, the groups compare their pictures, which can then be displayed in the class. Children who are deaf should receive written instructions, or the picture should be completed with students drawing one third of the body freely, without direction.

Figure 2.6. Group Picture

Additional Notes:

Guess the Animal

Equipment:	• Stopwatch
Location:	• Classroom, gymnasium, outdoors
Skill Development:	Large motor, following directions, visual perception, creative thinking
Abilities Required:	
Activity:	Children stand in circle formation with one person standing in the middle. The child in the middle spins around and, as he stops, points to someone in the circle. If there are children who are visually impaired in the group, the child's name should be said out loud. The child who is pointed to has 30 seconds to create an animal through body movement. If the child in the middle guesses the animal, he remains in the middle; if he does not, the person who was pointed to takes his place. If the student in the middle is blind, children should make the sound of the animal. Children in wheelchairs should also verbalize the sounds of the animals, unless the animals can be conveyed from a sitting position.

Figure 2.7. Guess the Animal

Additional Notes:

I Like People Who . . .

Equipment: • None

Location: • Classroom

Skill Development: Large motor, verbal communication, auditory processing, following directions

Abilities Required:

Activity: Children sit on chairs in circle formation. One child stands in the middle and starts the game by announcing, "I like people who . . ." and then completing the sentence with a comment of her choice, such as, "have brown hair," "like basketball," or "like playing video games." If leaders are non-verbal, they should demonstrate the appropriate actions. Everyone who is included in the statement gets up and looks for a new seat. Children in wheelchairs should move to another place in the circle. At the same time, the child in the middle attempts to find a chair to sit on. The child left without a seat becomes the new leader. She stands in the middle of the circle and makes a new statement about the type of people she likes. If there is only one child to whom the statement refers, that child automatically becomes the new leader. A portable sound source should be placed next to one of the empty chairs to assist children who are visually impaired.

Additional Notes: _____

                       _____

                       _____

                       _____

                       _____

                       _____

                       _____

                       _____

                       _____

                       _____

Introductions

Equipment:

- Index cards

- Pens

Location:

- Classroom

Skill Development: Large motor, verbal communication, auditory processing, creative thinking

Abilities Required:

Activity: This activity is most effective if carried out on the first day of class. Students write their names on index cards and are then put in pairs. The partners spend 2 minutes telling each other things about themselves. Students then switch name cards and find new partners. They then introduce themselves to their new partners as the person whose index card they have. The game continues in this fashion with children moving around the room introducing themselves as someone different each time. At the end of the game each pair should take turns introducing themselves in front of the group so that children can see how much of what is said about them is accurate. Blind children should be paired with sighted partners. This game can be played with non-verbal children who have the ability to write information received auditorily. If all children in the class are non-verbal or deaf, the game can be adapted by having children write information about themselves on the index cards and then exchanging cards with one other until their original cards are back in their possession.

Additional Notes: _____

_____

_____

_____

_____

_____

_____

_____

_____

_____

Pass the Beanbag

Equipment:	• Beanbag
	• Music source
Location:	• Classroom, gymnasium
Skill Development:	Fine motor, large motor, hand-eye coordination, following directions, visual perception, creative thinking

Abilities Required:

Activity: Children stand in circle formation. When the music starts, a beanbag is passed around the circle. When the music stops, the child holding the beanbag chooses an exercise, such as jumping jacks or running on the spot, for the class to copy. The exercise is performed until the music resumes. The teacher should try to stop the music when a different child has the beanbag each time, so that everyone has an opportunity to lead the group. Actions should be adapted accordingly for children in wheelchairs. For children who are blind, students should state the action they are performing. To assist children who are deaf, the teacher should wave a flag when the music stops.

Figure 2.8. Pass the Beanbag

Additional Notes:

Shaking Hands

Equipment:
- None

Location:
- Classroom, gymnasium, outdoors

Skill Development: Fine motor, large motor, following directions, academic

Abilities Required:

Activity: Children are assigned a number: one, two, or three. Everyone walks around the play area shaking hands with one another. If a child is a number one, he shakes other children's hands once. Children assigned number two shake twice, and those who are a number three shake three times. The object is to determine which children share the same number without talking. Once a child finds another player who shakes the same number of times, they stay together to find other players who are the same number. The game ends when all the ones, twos, and threes are in separate groups. To help students who are visually impaired locate them, children should use sound-makers. Children who are blind should be paired with sighted partners.

Additional Notes: _____
_____
_____
_____
_____
_____
_____
_____
_____
_____
_____
_____
_____
_____

World Traveler

Equipment:
- Large index cards
- Sheets of paper
- Tape
- Pens

Location:
- Classroom

Skill Development: Fine motor, large motor, visual perception, academic, verbal communication

Abilities Required:

Activity: This activity is good for any lesson where facts have to be memorized. If the topic is countries around the world, the name of a different country is taped to each child's back. The object of the game is for children to make lists of all the countries on everyone's backs. Children should not run or stand stationary to prevent other children from reading their countries. After a specific time period, the children sit down and read off their lists to the class. This activity can then be used to begin a review of material covered, such as asking children to locate the countries on maps. Children in wheelchairs should have the words taped to the back of their chairs.

Additional Notes: _____
_____
_____
_____
_____
_____
_____
_____
_____
_____
_____

Spell the Word

Equipment: • Paper

                 • Markers

                 • Scissors

                 • Envelopes

Location: • Classroom

Skill Development: Fine motor, visual perception, academic

Abilities Required:

Activity: Students are divided into groups of three. Each group has an envelope containing squares of paper with letters written on them. When placed in correct order, the squares spell a certain word. Each group should have a different word associated with a unit of study. The groups are told what topic their word relates to and on the go signal work together to sort the squares into the correct sequence. If students are studying animal kingdoms, for example, students may be told that their words are different classes of vertebrates. In this case, each group would have one of the following words to make: reptiles, mammals, birds, fishes, amphibians. For children who are visually impaired, letters should be at least 2 inches tall and printed in thick black ink on a white background. Braille writers should be used to imprint letters on the cards for children who are blind.

Figure 2.9. Spell the Word

Additional Notes:

Twenty Questions

Equipment:	• None
Location:	• Classroom
Skill Development:	Visual perception, auditory processing, verbal communication
Abilities Required:	

Activity:

One student is selected to be the leader and leaves the room. The rest of the children pick an object in the room that everyone can see. The leader returns to the group and must try to guess what the object is by asking questions that can be answered by "yes" or "no." For example, if the object is the chalkboard, and the child asks, "Is it on the floor?" the rest of the class would respond, "No." If the child asks, "Is it big?" the children would answer, "Yes." After 20 questions, the child can be given a clue. If she still does not guess correctly, clues can be given until she does. For children who are deaf, signals should be used to indicate yes or no. If the leader is blind, an object should be picked that is known to be in the room, like desks, chalkboard, or books.

Additional Notes:

_____

_____

_____

_____

_____

_____

_____

_____

_____

_____

_____

_____

_____

_____

Who's Your Neighbor?

Equipment:	• None
Location:	• Classroom
Skill Development:	Visual perception, auditory processing, verbal communication
Abilities Required:	

Activity: This activity is most effective if played on the first day of school or for children who interact very infrequently. Children are seated in circle formation with the leader standing in the middle. The leader approaches one of the children and says, "Hello I'm (Maria)," to which the child replies, "Hello, I'm (Brandon)." The leader then asks, "Who is the person to your right?" The child names the student next to him. If the child cannot name the student, he changes places with the child in the middle. If he answers correctly, the leader asks, "Who is the person to your left?" The student must again answer correctly to be able to stay in his seat. If a correct response is given to both questions, the leader sits down and another leader is chosen. For students who are visually impaired, children should use sound-makers. When the leader asks, "Who is the child to your right?" that child should jingle bells, squeeze a squeaky ball, or make another sound that will identify her to the child with visual impairments. This game can be played with children who are non-verbal if they have the ability to write or sign names.

Additional Notes:

_____

_____

_____

_____

_____

_____

_____

_____

_____

_____

Two Heads

Equipment:	• None
Location:	• Classroom, gymnasium, outdoors
Skill Development:	Large motor, hand-eye coordination, following directions, visual perception, auditory processing, creative thinking, academic
Abilities Required:	
Activity:	Children are divided into groups of four or five. The teacher calls out a command such as, "Three heads!" and the groups decide how they can respond so that three heads are being touched. They may decide that one child in the group touches two other heads and that one child touches her own head. If a command such as, "Four knees!" is called, two children in the group may touch both of their knees, or four children may touch one knee each. The game can be adapted for children with hearing impairments by indicating the body part and showing the number by holding up the corresponding number of fingers or a sign. Children with visual impairments should be paired with sighted partners.

Figure 2.10. Two Heads

Additional Notes:

_____

_____

_____

_____

_____

_____

_____

_____

_____

_____

_____

_____

_____

_____

_____

_____

_____

_____

_____

_____

_____

_____

_____

_____

_____

_____

_____

_____

_____

_____

_____

_____

_____

_____

_____

PART TWO

Gym and Outdoor Games

3

Gym and Outdoor Games

Level 1 Activities

Level 1 Gym and Outdoor Games

Level 1 Gym and Outdoor Games— By Skills

Animal Parade

Equipment: • None

Location: • Gymnasium, outdoors

Skill Development: Large motor, following directions, visual perception, creative thinking

Abilities Required:

Activity: Children are divided into groups of three or four. One child in each group is chosen to be the leader and the other children line up behind her. The leader picks an animal and then moves around the gym in this fashion. As a duck, for example, the child walks by crouching down with hands on hips and waddling from side to side. The other children follow the leader and copy his actions. When the leader makes the sound of the animal, the children copy this, too. Each child should have a turn leading the group. Children should wear sound-makers to assist children who are visually impaired, and the animal to be imitated should be stated out loud.

Figure 3.1. Animal Parade

Additional Notes:

Animal Tag

Equipment:	• None
Location:	• Gymnasium, outdoors
Skill Development:	Large motor, following directions, auditory processing, creative thinking
Abilities Required:	

Activity: One child is "It" and picks an animal for the children to move around the gym as. For example, if the child picks an elephant, everyone, including It, moves around the gym as an elephant. The child who is It chases the children, attempting to tag someone. When a child is tagged, the child who is It calls out, "Tag!" and everyone stops in their tracks. The tagged child then calls out the name of a new animal and children continue moving around the gym as this animal. When playing with children who are visually impaired, students should use sound-makers, and It should be identified by a different sound. Bell bracelets with Velcro fasteners can be worn on wrists or ankles and can be easily transferred from one child to another. The child who is It should wave a flag while calling "Tag" for children who are deaf.

Additional Notes: _____

_____

_____

_____

_____

_____

_____

_____

_____

_____

_____

_____

_____

Capture the Children

Equipment: • Parachute

Location: • Gymnasium, outdoors

Skill Development: Fine motor, large motor, following directions, auditory processing

Abilities Required:

Activity: Children stand in a circle, holding on to the edge of a parachute. Students begin by practicing how to lift and drop the parachute together. The teacher then calls out two names and these children run under the parachute and exchange places with each other. As they are running, the other children lower the parachute and attempt to capture them underneath. The aim is for each child to get to the other child's place before being trapped under the parachute. Children should attach bells to their ankles to assist children who are visually impaired, and a portable sound source should be placed in the spot left empty by the other child.

Additional Notes: _____

_____

_____

_____

_____

_____

_____

_____

_____

_____

_____

_____

_____

_____

Back to Back

Equipment: • Gym mats

Location: • Gymnasium, outdoors

Skill Development: Large motor, balancing

Abilities Required:

Activity: Children are divided into pairs and sit back to back with their knees bent and elbows linked. They then try to stand up together without falling over. When they can stand up from this position with ease, another child is added to the pair. Children then sit in a threesome, with arms linked. If the group manages to stand up as a three, another child is added. This continues with children being added to the group until all the children are in one large group.

Figure 3.2. Back to Back

Additional Notes:

Balloon Lift

Equipment: • Balloons

Location: • Gymnasium, outdoors

Skill Development: Large motor, hand-eye coordination, visual perception

Abilities Required:

Activity: Children are divided into groups of four or five and stand in circle forma-
                        tion. Each group has a balloon that they toss into the air. The object of the
                        game is to pass the balloon around the circle while keeping it airborne for
                        as long as possible. Children should use all body parts, including their
                        heads, arms, hands, and legs to keep the balloon in the air while passing
                        it around the circle to each member of the group. A small bell can be at-
                        tached to the balloon to assist children who are visually impaired.

Figure 3.3. Balloon Lift

Additional Notes:

_____
_____
_____
_____
_____
_____
_____
_____
_____
_____
_____
_____
_____
_____
_____
_____
_____
_____
_____
_____
_____
_____
_____
_____
_____
_____
_____
_____
_____
_____
_____
_____

Beanbag Catch

Equipment: • Beanbags

Location: • Gymnasium, outdoors

Skill Development: Fine motor, large motor, hand-eye coordination, visual perception

Abilities Required:

Activity: Children stand in pairs facing each other a few feet apart. On a given signal, one child in each pair throws a beanbag to her partner. If the partner catches it, she takes one step backward and then throws it back from this new position. If the beanbag is not caught by her partner, both players stay where they are. The object of the game is to move farther apart with each throw. When children reach the farthest point at which the beanbag can be caught, they play beanbag catch. For children who are visually impaired, larger, brightly colored beanbags should be used. Beepers can also be inserted into beanbags or foam balls for children who are blind. An aide should be available to pick up beanbags dropped by children in wheelchairs.

Figure 3.4. Beanbag Catch

Additional Notes:

Blob Tag

Equipment: • None

Location: • Gymnasium, outdoors

Skill Development: Large motor, visual perception

Abilities Required:

Activity: One child is the "blob" and chases the other children around the gym. When the blob tags someone, they join hands and run around together. The two children then try to tag someone else and that child joins the pair. The game continues in this way with children trying to tag other children to add to the blob. When everyone has been caught, the whole group runs around the gym as one big blob. For children who are visually impaired, children should wear bells attached to their ankles. The blob should be identified by a different sound. When forming blobs with children in wheelchairs, children should hold on to the handles of the chairs.

Figure 3.5. Blob Tag

Additional Notes:

Catch the Dragon's Tail

Equipment:	• Handkerchiefs
Location:	• Gymnasium, outdoors
Skill Development:	Fine motor, large motor, hand-eye coordination, visual perception
Abilities Required:	

Activity: Children are divided into teams, each pretending to be a dragon. In each group, children stand behind one another and hold on to the waist of the person in front. The first child in each line is the dragon's head, and the last person is the dragon's tail. A handkerchief is placed in the back pocket of the dragon's tail. Dragons chase one another around the gym, trying to snatch the handkerchiefs from the other dragons' tails. The game ends when the last dragon has the handkerchief removed from his tail. Children who are blind should be placed in groups with sighted children.

Additional Notes:
_____
_____
_____
_____
_____
_____
_____
_____
_____
_____
_____
_____
_____
_____
_____

Centipedes

Equipment: • None

Location: • Gymnasium, outdoors

Skill Development: Large motor

Abilities Required:

Activity: Children pretend to be centipedes by lining up in groups of three and holding on to the waist of the child standing in front of them. One child is on his own and as the centipedes run around the gym, he chases them and tries to attach himself to the last child in any group. This newly formed centipede then runs around and tries to attach itself to the end of another centipede. The game continues in this fashion until all the children are running around the gym as one giant centipede. Visually impaired students should be grouped with sighted children.

Figure 3.6. Centipede

Additional Notes:

Drop the Handkerchief

Equipment:	• Handkerchief
Location:	• Gymnasium, outdoors
Skill Development:	Fine motor, large motor
Abilities Required:	

Activity: Children stand in circle formation. One child walks around the outside of the circle and drops a handkerchief behind someone. The child it lands behind picks up the handkerchief and chases the other child around the circle. The handkerchief dropper tries to run back to the other child's place in the circle without being caught. If he succeeds, the child who was chasing him becomes the new handkerchief dropper. If caught, the child remains the handkerchief dropper for the next round. For children who are visually impaired, a brightly colored handkerchief or beeper ball should be used and the name of the child should be said out loud. The handkerchief dropper should also wear bells on her ankles or use another sound-maker as she is running. An aide should be available to pick up handkerchiefs for children in wheelchairs.

Additional Notes: _____

_____

_____

_____

_____

_____

_____

_____

_____

_____

_____

_____

Follow the Leader

Equipment: Various gym apparatus such as:

                         • Mats, benches, box horses, skipping ropes

Location: • Gymnasium

Skill Development: Large motor, following directions, visual perception

Abilities Required:

Activity: The teacher sets up an obstacle course in the gym and divides the children into groups of three or four. Each group has a leader, and the other children line up behind him and follow his actions. The leader tries to keep the line in motion by moving in different ways while leading the group through the obstacle course. Actions may include jumping up, hopping, skipping, and walking backwards. When all the groups have completed the obstacle course, the child behind the leader becomes the new leader and the original leader goes to the end of the line. Fluorescent tape should be attached to apparatus for children who are visually impaired, and children should wear sound-makers. Blind students should be paired with sighted aides.

Additional Notes: _____

                         _____

                         _____

                         _____

                         _____

                         _____

                         _____

                         _____

                         _____

                         _____

                         _____

                         _____

Grab the Flag

Equipment:	• Pieces of cloth (or handkerchiefs)
Location:	• Gymnasium, outdoors
Skill Development:	Fine motor, large motor, hand-eye coordination
Abilities Required:	

Activity: Each child has a piece of cloth (a flag) hanging from her waistband or back pocket. The object of the game is for children to run around the gym and snatch as many flags as they can from other players, while trying to prevent theirs from being taken. Children may not touch their own flags and can stop them from being grabbed only by moving out of other children's reach. At any time, the teacher can call a "break," at which point all the flags are returned to the original owners and the game begins again. For students who are visually impaired, children should wear bells attached to their ankles and brightly colored pieces of cloth should be used. Children in wheelchairs should have flags tucked into the back of their chairs so that they can be easily removed.

Figure 3.7. Grab the Flag

Additional Notes:

Jump and Jump Again

Equipment:	• None
Location:	• Gymnasium, outdoors
Skill Development:	Large motor
Abilities Required:	

Activity: Children are divided into groups of five or six and stand at one end of the gym. The object of the game is for children to jump collectively as far as possible. The first child begins by making the longest jump that he can. All the children in the group walk to where he lands and the next child starts her jump from that point. This is repeated until children reach the end of the gym. The aim is for children to get to the opposite end of the gym with as few jumps as possible, trying to better their collective distance each time. Children who are blind should be grouped with sighted students.

Figure 3.8. Jump and Jump Again

Additional Notes:

Moving Circle

Equipment:	• None
Location:	• Gymnasium, outdoors
Skill Development:	Large motor, balancing
Abilities Required:	
Activity:	Children stand in circle formation, spaced evenly apart. They then turn 90 degrees in a clockwise direction and crouch down as if sitting on invisible chairs. When everyone is stable in this position, each child takes a step back and sits on the lap of the child behind. When all the children have their weight on the person behind them, the group tries to move the same foot at the same time and walk around in a circle. Verbal directions should be given for children who are blind.
Additional Notes:	

_____

_____

_____

_____

_____

_____

_____

_____

_____

_____

_____

_____

_____

_____

_____

_____

Numbers

Equipment: • None

Location: • Gymnasium, outdoors

Skill Development: Large motor, auditory processing, academic, following directions

Abilities Required:

Activity: Children run around the gym in the same direction. When the teacher calls a number, such as "Three!" children form groups of three with the children standing closest to them. They then link arms to show that they are in a group. Only numbers that form an even number of groups should be called. On a given signal, children continue running around the gym. If "One!" is called, children stop in their tracks until given the signal to continue running. Children who are blind should be paired with a sighted partner. For children who are hearing impaired, the numbers should be displayed on construction paper and held in front of children as they are running around the gym.

Figure 3.9. Numbers

Additional Notes:

Tag the Number

Equipment: • None

Location: • Gymnasium, outdoors

Skill Development: Large motor, auditory processing, following directions

Abilities Required:

Activity: Children stand in circle formation and are numbered off, one through four, so that each child has a number. The teacher calls out a number, such as "Two," at which point all the twos break away from the group and run around the circle in a clockwise direction. The object of the game is for children to tag the person running in front of them before she gets back to her place. Children should wear bells around their ankles as they are running to assist students who are visually impaired. The teacher should hold up signs with numbers written on them or indicate the numbers with fingers for children who are deaf.

Additional Notes: _____

_____

_____

_____

_____

_____

_____

_____

_____

_____

_____

_____

_____

_____

_____

_____

Partner Tag

Equipment:	• None
Location:	• Gymnasium, outdoors
Skill Development:	Large motor, following directions
Abilities Required:	
Activity:	Children are divided into pairs. One player in each pair is "It" and can tag only his partner. Children run around the play area, with It in each pair chasing the partner. When a child is tagged, she becomes It and the roles are reversed. However, before running, the child counts to three to give her partner some time to escape. Each child should have a different sound-maker to assist students who are visually impaired. Children who are blind should be paired with sighted partners. Children with wheelchairs should be paired together or placed with ambulatory children who can push their chairs.
Additional Notes:	

Partner Pull-Up

Equipment: • Gym mats

Location: • Gymnasium

Skill Development: Fine motor, large motor, hand-eye coordination, balancing

Abilities Required:

Activity: Children are in pairs and sit facing each other with their legs bent at the knees and the soles of their feet flat on the floor. Then they lean forward, bending their knees as much as necessary, and grasp hands. By evenly distributing their weight and pulling together, they stand up. Once this is mastered, children can team up with other pairs and attempt a "pull-up" in groups of four. Children should also try returning to sitting positions without letting go of their partners' hands. Children who are blind should be paired with sighted partners.

Figure 3.10. Partner Pull-Up

Additional Notes:

Round and Around

Equipment: • Gym mats

Location: • Gymnasium

Skill Development: Large motor, following directions

Abilities Required:

Activity: Children lie in a large circle on their backs with their heads toward the
                       center. One child starts the game by getting up and running around the
                       outside of the circle. When she arrives back in her place, the child to the
                       right of her gets up and runs around. This process is repeated until every-
                       one in the group has had a turn to run. Children should use sound-
                       makers while running to assist children who are visually impaired. The
                       names of children who are blind should be said out loud when it is their
                       turn to run. If there are children in wheelchairs, the game should be
                       played with children sitting in chairs, rather than lying on their backs.

Figure 3.11. Round and Around

Additional Notes:

_____

_____

_____

_____

_____

_____

_____

_____

_____

_____

_____

_____

_____

_____

_____

_____

_____

_____

_____

_____

_____

_____

_____

_____

_____

_____

_____

_____

_____

_____

_____

Slithering Snake

Equipment:	• Gym mats
Location:	• Gymnasium
Skill Development:	Fine motor, large motor
Abilities Required:	 
Activity:	Children are divided into pairs and pretend to be snakes by lying on their stomachs and holding the ankles of the person in front of them. The "snakes" slither around the floor in pairs with the first child leading the way and the second child moving behind without losing grip of her partner's ankles. The first child in each pair slithers up to another snake and takes hold of the ankles of the second person in that pair to make a four-person snake. This group then tries to attach itself to another pair. The game continues in this way until the entire group forms one long snake. Blind children should be paired with sighted partners.

Figure 3.12. Slithering Snake

Additional Notes:

Swaying Scarf

Equipment:	• Strips of colored material
	• Music source
Location:	• Gymnasium
Skill Development:	Fine motor, large motor, auditory processing, following directions
Abilities Required:	

Activity: Children are divided into pairs or small groups, each with a long strip of colored material. Each child holds on to part of the material as the groups move around the room to music. The teacher gives instructions as to how the groups should move, such as running, skipping, or jumping, while holding the scarf high, low, or behind them. Children follow the directions of the teacher while moving the scarf accordingly as a group. For children who are hearing impaired, the teacher should demonstrate the actions to be performed. Children who are blind should be placed in groups with sighted children. If there are students in wheelchairs, directions should be adapted accordingly.

Figure 3.13. Swaying Scarf

Additional Notes:

_____

_____

_____

_____

_____

_____

_____

_____

_____

_____

_____

_____

_____

_____

_____

_____

_____

_____

_____

_____

_____

_____

_____

_____

_____

_____

_____

_____

_____

_____

_____

_____

Gym and Outdoor Games

Level 2 Activities

Level 2 Gym and Outdoor Games

Level 2 Gym and Outdoor Games— by Skills

Following Directions

Visual Perception

Verbal Communication

Academic

Creative Thinking

Balancing

Action Tag

Equipment:	• None
Location:	• Gymnasium, outdoors
Skill Development:	Large motor, auditory processing, following directions
Abilities Required:	

Activity:

Children are divided into two groups and line up against opposing walls. One child, who is "It," stands in the middle and tries to tag children as they cross the gym in both directions. The child who is It calls out a movement, such as "Skip!" and all children skip to the other side of the gym, trying not to be tagged by It. The child who is It must also skip while attempting to tag the children. When children are tagged, they immediately become Its and try to tag others, while the original It skips as quickly as possible to the nearest wall. Children should use sound-makers while running to assist children who are visually impaired. The child who is It should be identified by a different type of sound. Children who are blind should be paired with sighted partners. Children with visual impairments may also benefit from noise generated by a portable sound source located at the other end of the gym. The child who is It should demonstrate the action to be performed for children who are deaf.

Additional Notes:

Alphabet Relay

Equipment: • Alphabet flash cards

Location: • Gymnasium, classroom

Skill Development: Fine motor, large motor, academic, visual perception

Abilities Required:

Activity: Children are divided into two teams and line up in single file at one end
                        of the gym. A set of shuffled alphabet cards is placed about 20 feet from
                        each team. Letters should be laid out five at a time, starting with A
                        through E. On the go signal, the first player in each team runs to the pile
                        of cards and finds the letter A. The child then places the A on the floor
                        next to the pile, runs back and tags the next player in line. This child then
                        runs to the pile and finds the letter B and places it next to the A card. The
                        game continues in this manner until the whole alphabet is laid out in cor-
                        rect order. Letters should be at least 2 inches high and printed in thick
                        black ink on white backgrounds for children with visual impairments.
                        For children who are blind, letters should be imprinted on the cards us-
                        ing a braille-writer. Blind children should be paired with sighted chil-
                        dren when running to the pile of cards, or a portable sound source should
                        be placed next to the pile. Children in wheelchairs should have a portion
                        of the cards placed on a tray attached to their chairs.

Additional Notes: _____

                        _____

                        _____

                        _____

                        _____

                        _____

                        _____

                        _____

                        _____

                        _____

                        _____

Beanbag Dash

Equipment:	• Beanbags
Location:	• Gymnasium, outdoors
Skill Development:	Fine motor, large motor, hand-eye coordination
Abilities Required:	

Activity: Children are divided into two teams. Each team stands in single file, and the last player in each line is given a beanbag. On the go signal, the child with the beanbag runs to the front of the line, stands with his back facing the first child, and passes the beanbag to him over his head. The beanbag is passed in this way to the last player in line. This player runs to the front of the line and passes the beanbag back down the line. The game ends when the child who was originally last in line is back at the end of the line. A brightly colored beanbag should be used for children who are visually impaired. Children who are blind should be placed in groups with sighted children, and a portable sound source should be placed at the front of the line.

Additional Notes: _____

_____

_____

_____

_____

_____

_____

_____

_____

_____

_____

_____

_____

_____

Ball and Bottle Relay

Equipment: • Soda bottles

                        • Ping-Pong balls

Location: • Gymnasium, outdoors

Skill Development: Fine motor, large motor, hand-eye coordination

Abilities Required:

Activity: Children line up in two teams on one side of the gym. As many soda bottles as there are children on each team are placed 6 feet apart in a vertical line in front of each team. The first child in line runs with a Ping-Pong ball and places it on the mouth of the first bottle. The child then runs back to the end of his team's line and the next child in line runs to the first bottle, picks up the Ping-Pong ball, and places it on the second bottle. This child then runs back to the end of the line. The third child in line takes the ball from the second bottle and places it on the third. This is repeated until the ball is on the last bottle, at which point the child brings it back to the team. To assist children with visual impairments, Ping-Pong balls should be painted with brightly colored ink and bottles striped with fluorescent tape. Also, a portable sound source should be placed beside the first bottle, and bottles should be placed next to each other, rather than spaced apart. Children who are blind should be paired with sighted partners.

Figure 4.1. Ball and Bottle Relay

Additional Notes:

Beanbag Balance

Equipment: • Beanbags

Location: • Gymnasium, outdoors

Skill Development: Large motor, balancing

Abilities Required:

Activity: Children are divided into two equal-sized teams and line up on one side
                        of the gym. The first player in each team places a beanbag on her head
                        and, on the go signal, runs to a designated point. Children may not use
                        their hands to keep the beanbag in place. If the beanbag falls off, they
                        must place it back on their heads before running any farther. When the
                        first player returns to her original position, she hands the beanbag to the
                        next player in line, who then runs with the beanbag balanced on his head.
                        The game ends when all players have had a turn to run. For children who
                        are blind, one portable sound source should be located at the designated
                        finish point and another one, with a different pitch, should be located by
                        the team members. An aide should be available to pick up beanbags for
                        children in wheelchairs.

Figure 4.2. Beanbag Balance

Additional Notes:

Beanbag Relay

Equipment: • Beanbag

Location: • Gymnasium, outdoors

Skill Development: Fine motor, large motor, hand-eye coordination

Abilities Required:

Activity: Children stand an arm's length apart in a horizontal line. One child is the leader and stands facing them. She begins the game by throwing a beanbag to the child on the far left of the line. This child passes the beanbag to the child next to her who then passes it to the child next to her. When the last player receives the beanbag, she runs and takes the leader's place. At the same time, the leader runs and stands at the far left of the group. The game ends when this child is back in the leader position. For children who are visually impaired, beepers should be inserted into the beanbags, or beeper balls should be used. Also, children's names should be said out loud when the beanbag is being thrown to them.

Additional Notes: _____

_____

_____

_____

_____

_____

_____

_____

_____

_____

_____

_____

_____

Buzzing Flies

Equipment:	• Gym mats or clean floor
	• Whistle
Location:	Gymnasium, outdoors
Skill Development:	Large motor, visual perception
Abilities Required:	

Activity: Children are divided into two groups in a small play area. One group sits scattered around the floor, and are the "traps." The other children are "flies" who run around the room and "buzz" around the traps. When a whistle is blown, the flies freeze on the spot. If a trap can reach a fly with any part of her body, the fly sits down next to the trap and helps to catch the other flies. The game continues until all the flies have been caught. Traps can catch children with wheelchairs by touching any part of their chairs. For children who are hearing impaired, a flag should be waved as the stop signal. Markers, such as pylons, should be placed around the outside of the circle to assist children who are visually impaired. Children who are blind should be paired with sighted guides.

Additional Notes:

British Bulldog

Equipment:	• None
Location:	• Gymnasium, outdoors
Skill Development:	Large motor, auditory processing, following directions
Abilities Required:	
Activity:	Children line up at one end of the gym, with one child standing in the middle of the play area. When this child calls out, "Bulldog!" the children try to run to the other end of the gym without being tagged. Anyone who is tagged joins in trying to tag the other children. The game ends when everyone has been tagged. Children should use sound-makers while running to assist children with visual impairments, and the tagger should be identified by a different sound. Children who are blind should be paired with sighted partners. For students who are deaf, the child in the middle should wave a flag or use a signal while calling out, "Bulldog!"

Figure 4.3. British Bulldog

Additional Notes:

Blindfold Tag

Materials:	• Blindfold
Location:	• Gymnasium, outdoors
Skill Development:	Large motor, auditory processing, following directions, verbal communication

Abilities Required:

Activity: Children stand in circle formation and are numbered off consecutively. One child is "It" and stands in the middle of the circle, blindfolded. The child who is It calls out two numbers, and the children with those numbers exchange places with each other by running across the circle. The blindfolded player tries to tag the children as they switch places. If a child is tagged during the switch, he exchanges places with It. The blindfolded player may also call out three or four numbers, which would give him a better chance of tagging someone. Children should use sound-makers while running to assist children who are visually impaired, and the blindfolded player should be identified by a different sound. The child in the middle should hold up signs or use fingers to indicate the numbers for children who are deaf. Children in wheelchairs can be tagged by having any part of their chairs touched.

Additional Notes: _____

_____

_____

_____

_____

_____

_____

_____

_____

_____

_____

_____

_____

Catch the Frog

Equipment:	• Chalk
Location:	• Gymnasium, outdoors
Skill Development:	Large motor
Abilities Required:	

Activity:

Large circles are drawn on the ground and are the witches' "cooking pots." Two children are "witches" while all the others are "frogs" who try to run away from the witches to avoid being placed in one of their pots. The witches chase the frogs around the gym. When a child is caught, she is taken to a pot where she stands with her arms outstretched. Another frog can rescue a captured frog by grabbing hold of one of her hands. If a witch tags a frog in the act of saving another frog, this child is added to the cooking pot. The game ends when all the frogs have been caught. Children who are frogs should use sound-makers, and witches should be identified by different sounds to assist children with visual impairments. Children who are blind should be paired with sighted partners. The size of the circles should be large enough to accommodate all the children in wheelchairs.

Figure 4.4. Catch the Frog

Additional Notes:

Run, Number One

Equipment:	• None
Location:	• Gymnasium, outdoors
Skill Development:	Large motor, auditory processing, following directions
Abilities Required:	

Activity: Children stand at one end of the gym and are numbered off one through four. One child, who is the leader, stands in the middle of the gym. When she calls, "Run, number one," all the children who are ones run to the other end of the gym. As they pass the leader, they touch her hand. The last child to touch the leader's hand becomes the new leader and the leader takes on that child's number. The leader may also ask two groups to run, in which case she would call out, "Run, numbers two and four." Children should use sound-makers while running to assist children who are visually impaired. The numbers should be indicated using a sign or fingers to assist children who are deaf. Children in wheelchairs should be given the same numbers as one another.

Additional Notes: _____

_____

_____

_____

_____

_____

_____

_____

_____

_____

_____

_____

_____

Sack Relay

Equipment:	• Burlap sacks
Location:	• Gymnasium, outdoors
Skill Development:	Large motor

Abilities Required:

Activity: Children are divided into equal-sized teams and line up on one side of the gym. The first player on each team steps into a sack. On the go signal, the children in the sacks jump to a finish line and back again. They then step out of the sacks and hand them to the next players in line, who in turn jump in the sacks to the finish line and back to the next player in line. The game is over when the last player on each team is back with his group. Portable sound sources should be placed near the teams and by the finish line to assist children who are visually impaired.

Additional Notes:

_____

_____

_____

_____

_____

_____

_____

_____

_____

_____

_____

_____

_____

_____

_____

_____

_____

Catch the Mice

Equipment:	• None
Location:	• Gymnasium, outdoors
Skill Development:	Large motor, auditory processing, following directions
Abilities Required:	
Activity:	Children are divided into two groups. One group is the "mousetrap" and the rest of the children are "mice." The mousetrap stands in circle formation with hands joined. The mice are scattered around the outside of the circle. When the teacher calls, "Trap's open!" the children who are the mousetrap lift their arms and the mice begin to run underneath, in and out of the circle. When "Trap's shut!" is called, the mousetrap children put their arms down and all those caught inside the circle become new members of the trap. The game continues until all the mice are caught. Children who are part of the trap should wear bells attached to their wrists to assist children who are visually impaired. The teacher should wave a flag while calling "Trap's open!" for children who are deaf. Children in wheelchairs should be part of the mousetrap.

Figure 4.5. Catch the Mice

Additional Notes:

Cats and Dogs

Equipment: • None

Location: • Gymnasium, outdoors

Skill Development: Large motor, auditory processing, following directions

Abilities Required:

Activity: Children are divided into two groups, one being the "cats" and the other the "dogs." The groups stand a few feet apart with their backs to each other. A marker should be placed 30 feet in front of each team, indicating the safety base. When the teacher calls "Cats," or "Dogs," that team runs forward, while the other team turns around and tries to catch them before they reach their safety base. Any child caught joins the other team for the next round. A portable sound source should be placed at the safety base to assist children who are visually impaired. The teacher should stand in front of children who are deaf and use a signal, such as waving a flag, to indicate their turn to run.

Figure 4.6. Cats and Dogs

Additional Notes:

Copy Cat Relay

Equipment:
- None

Location:
- Gymnasium, outdoors

Skill Development: Large motor, following directions, balancing

Abilities Required:

Activity: Children are divided into equal-sized teams and line up on one side of the gym. The first player in each team picks an action such as hopping or jumping and moves to a designated point and back using this action. The next player in line repeats the action. The relay continues in this fashion until all children have had a turn to "run" using the chosen movement. Actions should be verbally stated for children who are visually impaired and portable sound sources should be placed next to the finish line and the team.

Additional Notes: _____

_____

_____

_____

_____

_____

_____

_____

_____

_____

_____

_____

_____

_____

_____

_____

Knights

Equipment:	• Hula hoop
	• "Sword" made of rolled-up newspaper
Location:	• Gymnasium, outdoors
Skill Development:	Large motor, following directions

Abilities Required:

 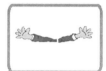

Activity: Children stand in large circle formation with a hula hoop in the middle. One child, who is "It," walks around the inside of the circle and "knights" someone by touching her on the shoulder with a paper sword. The child who is It then runs to the hula hoop and drops the sword in it. The child who was knighted runs to the hula hoop at the same time, picks up the sword, and tries to tag It with it before he can run back to the empty spot in the circle. If successful, the child returns to her original place. If unsuccessful, she becomes It and knights another player with the sword. A portable sound source should be placed in the hula hoop to assist children who are visually impaired, and the sword should be covered with brightly colored construction paper. The child who is It should use a sound-maker while running, such as bells attached to wrists or ankles, which can be easily transferred from one child to another.

Additional Notes:
_____
_____
_____
_____
_____
_____
_____
_____
_____
_____
_____

Farm Animal Relay

Equipment:	• None
Location:	• Gymnasium
Skill Development:	Large motor, following directions, visual perception, creative thinking
Abilities Required:	
Activity:	Children are divided into equal-sized teams and line up at one end of the gym. Each group picks a farm animal, such as a chicken, sheep, or horse. The first child in each group crawls to the other end of the gym and back in the manner of the animal chosen. When the first player returns, the next child in line repeats the process. The game continues in this fashion until all members of the team have had a turn. Verbal directions should be given to children who are visually impaired, and portable sound sources should be placed by the team and at the other end of the gym. Children who are blind should be paired with sighted partners.

Figure 4.7. Farm Animal Relay

Additional Notes:

Fire in the Forest!

Equipment:	• None
Location:	• Gymnasium, outdoors
Skill Development:	Large motor, auditory processing, following directions, verbal communication
Abilities Required:	

Activity: Children are divided into two groups and stand in double circle formation. The outer circle has one more child than the inner circle, who are "trees." One child stands in the middle and when he calls out, "Fire in the forest—run! run!" the children in the outer circle run in a clockwise direction while the trees remain still. When the child shouts, "Fire's out!" children stop in their tracks and place their hands on the shoulders of the person standing in front of them in the inner circle. There will be one child without a tree. This child stands in the middle of the circle and becomes the caller for the next game and the original caller joins the outer circle. Children who are blind should run with sighted partners. A flag should be waved or another signal used to indicate the run prompt for children who are deaf.

Additional Notes: _____

_____

_____

_____

_____

_____

_____

_____

_____

_____

_____

Fishes and Whales

Equipment:	• None
Location:	• Gymnasium, outdoors
Skill Development:	Large motor, auditory processing, following directions, verbal communication
Abilities Required:	

Activity:

Children are divided into two groups, "fishes" and "whales." Groups stand facing each other on opposite sides of the gym. One child is the "Big Octopus" and stands in between the two groups. The Big Octopus may call out, "Fishes" or "Whales," either separately or together. The object is for the fishes and whales to get to the opposite side of the gym without being tagged by the octopus. Children who are tagged sit down and help the octopus from a sitting position. The game continues until all the children are sitting. Children should wear sound-makers while running, and the Big Octopus should be identified by a different type of sound to assist children who are visually impaired. Children who are blind should be paired with sighted partners. For children who are deaf, either large pictures of fishes or whales should be held up, or signals used to indicate which group should run. When students in wheelchairs are caught, they should remain stationary while attempting to tag other children.

Additional Notes:

_____

_____

_____

_____

_____

_____

_____

_____

_____

_____

_____

_____

Guard the Moon

Equipment:
• Chalk

Location:
• Gymnasium, outdoors

Skill Development:
Large motor, visual perception, following directions

Abilities Required:

Activity:
A large circle is drawn on the ground to indicate the moon. Three children stand inside the circle and protect the moon from invasion by tagging players who enter the circle. Students cannot step outside the circle to tag. The rest of the children are "earthlings" who try to get inside the circle without being tagged. Children who land on the moon with both feet without being tagged are safe and remain inside the circle. They then help the moon people by tagging other children who enter the circle. Fluorescent tape should be used around the edge of the circle to assist children who are visually impaired. Children should also use sound-makers while tagging. Children who are blind should be paired with sighted partners. Moon children can tag children in wheelchairs by touching any part of their chairs.

Figure 4.8. Guard the Moon

Additional Notes:

Freeze Tag

Equipment:	• None
Location:	• Gymnasium, outdoors
Skill Development:	Large motor, auditory processing, following directions, verbal communication

Abilities Required:

Activity:

Children stand in a horizontal line at one end of the gym. One child, who is "It," stands in the middle of the play area. When he calls, "Just try it!" children try to run across the gym without being tagged. If the child who is It does tag them, they freeze on the spot. When It calls "Just try it!" again, the children who are not frozen turn around and run back to the other side of the gym. As they are running, they have to avoid the frozen players, who can also tag them. Only It can run—the frozen players must tag children from their standing positions. Children should wear sound-makers and the child who is It should be identified by a different sound to assist children who are visually impaired. Portable sound sources should be placed at both ends of the gym. Children who are blind should be paired with sighted partners. The child who is It should wave a flag while calling, "Just try it!" for children who are deaf. Children in wheelchairs can be tagged by having any part of their chairs touched.

Additional Notes: _____

_____

_____

_____

_____

_____

_____

_____

_____

_____

Freezers

Equipment:	• Arm bands
Location:	• Gymnasium, outdoors
Skill Development:	Large motor, following directions

Abilities Required:

Activity: Children run around the gym. There are three or four children who are "freezers" and who try to tag them. Freezers should wear arm bands so that they can be identified by the other children. When a child is tagged he must "freeze" with legs astride and stay in this position until another child unfreezes him by crawling under his legs. After a child has crawled under his legs, the frozen child is free to run around again. Children should wear sound-makers, and freezers should be identified by a different type of sound to assist children who are visually impaired. Children who are blind should be paired with sighted partners.

Additional Notes: _____

_____

_____

_____

_____

_____

_____

_____

_____

_____

_____

_____

_____

_____

Link Arms

Equipment:	• None
Location:	• Gymnasium, outdoors
Skill Development:	Large motor, following directions
Abilities Required:	
Activity:	Children run around the play area in pairs, with arms linked. Two children are not linked. One of them is "It" and tries to tag her partner. The child who is being chased must link up with any other pair to avoid being tagged by It. The child on the other side of the pair then breaks off, and is chased by It. If caught, this child becomes the new It, and the original It runs off and tries to find a pair to link arms with. Players should use sound-makers while running to assist children who are visually impaired. Children who are blind should be paired with sighted partners. Children in wheelchairs should be paired with ambulatory partners, who should push the chairs rather than run with arms linked.

Figure 4.9. Link Arms

Additional Notes:

Mirror, Mirror

Equipment:	• None
Locations:	• Gymnasium, outdoors
Skill Development:	Large motor, following directions, visual perception
Abilities Required:	

Activity: Children move freely around the gym. When the teacher calls, "Partners!" children pair up with the players standing closest to them. The children then number themselves one and two, or are assigned numbers by the teacher. The pairs stand facing each other and, on a given signal, child number one acts out a movement that her partner copies, pretending to be the mirror. The mime continues until the teacher calls out, "Switch!" at which point the roles are reversed. On the go signal, children continue moving around the gym until "Partners" is called again, at which point children pair up with different partners and perform other mimes. Children should use sound-makers while running to assist children who are visually impaired and actions should be verbally stated. Students should adapt their movements accordingly when paired with children in wheelchairs.

Figure 4.10. Mirror, Mirror

Additional Notes:

Non-Stop Relay

Equipment:	• Chalk
Location:	• Gymnasium, outdoors
Skill Development:	Large motor, following directions
Abilities Required:	

Activity: Children are divided into two teams and line up in single file on one side of the gym. One child in each team stands facing the group on a line about 25 feet away. On the go signal, this child runs to the first player in her team. She grabs that player by the hand and they both run back to the line. Then the child who was the first player in line runs back and gets the second player. The game ends when all children are on the other side of the line. Children who are blind should be placed in groups with sighted children. Children should push students in wheelchairs or run next to them, rather than hold their hands.

Additional Notes:

_____

_____

_____

_____

_____

_____

_____

_____

_____

_____

_____

_____

_____

_____

_____

_____

Pick Up a Buddy!

Equipment: • Pylons

Location: • Gymnasium, outdoors

Skill Development: Large motor, following directions

Abilities Required:

Activity: Pylons are arranged in circle formation around the gym, with one child standing at each one. One child stands a few feet away from the first pylon. She begins the game by running to the first child and holding hands with this child as they run together to the next station. The child from the first pylon then joins hands with the child from the second pylon and as a threesome, they run to the third pylon. The game continues until all the children have been picked up and arrive back at the starting position in one group. Pylons should be striped with fluorescent tape to assist children who are visually impaired. Students should hold on to the handles of wheelchairs, rather than children's hands.

Additional Notes: _____

_____

_____

_____

_____

_____

_____

_____

_____

_____

_____

_____

_____

_____

Otter and Seagull

Equipment:	• None
Location:	• Gymnasium, outdoors
Skill Development:	Large motor, following directions
Abilities Required:	

Activity:

Children are divided into pairs, one standing behind the other with their hands on their partner's shoulders. These children are the "nests." There are two children who are not in a pair, one being the seagull and the other the otter. The otter chases the seagull around the play area. To escape being caught, the seagull hides in one of the nests. When the seagull runs under the children's arms, the child who forms the front of the nest breaks away from her partner and the seagull takes her place. The child who breaks away becomes a seagull and is now chased by the otter. If the otter catches her before she reaches another nest, the roles become reversed and the seagull chases the otter. Students should use sound-makers while running to assist children who are visually impaired. Children who are blind should have a sighted guide. Children in wheelchairs should be the front of the nest.

Figure 4.11. Otter and Seagull

Additional Notes:

Rhyming Circle

Equipment:	• None
Location:	• Gymnasium, outdoors
Skill Development:	Large motor, auditory processing, following directions

Abilities Required:

Activity: Children stand in large circle formation and are numbered off one through four. There should be at least two children of each number. The object of the game is for children to run around the circle and back to their places when they hear words that rhyme with their numbers. The teacher should go over some examples before beginning the game, such as "One, fun, sun," "Two, shoe, blue," "Three, flea, bee," and "Four, door, more." Children run when they hear a word that rhymes with their number, and when the last child is back in her place, a new word is called. Markers, such as pylons, should be placed around the outside of the circle to assist children who are visually impaired, and children should use sound-makers while running. Children who are blind should be placed next to sighted partners with the same numbers.

Additional Notes:

Running Numbers

Equipment:	• None
Location:	• Gymnasium, outdoors
Skill Development:	Large motor, auditory processing, following directions
Abilities Required:	
Activity:	Children sit in two equal lines facing each other a few feet apart. Each child is paired with the player sitting opposite him and the pairs are numbered off starting at one. When the teacher calls a number, the children with that number stand up, run up the outside of their lines, and back down the middle to their starting positions. When both the children are seated, the first child back calls out the number of the next pair to run. Portable sound sources should be placed at both ends of the line to assist children who are visually impaired and verbal directions can also be given. Children who are blind should run with sighted partners. The teacher should hold up signs with numbers written on them, or indicate the number using fingers, for children who are deaf.

Figure 4.12. Running Numbers

Additional Notes:

_____

_____

_____

_____

_____

_____

_____

_____

_____

_____

_____

_____

_____

_____

_____

_____

_____

_____

_____

_____

_____

_____

_____

_____

_____

_____

_____

_____

_____

_____

_____

_____

_____

Shirt Button Relay

Equipment:	• Shirts
Location:	• Gymnasium, classroom
Skill Development:	Fine motor, large motor, hand-eye coordination, visual perception

Abilities Required:

Activity: Children are divided into equal-sized teams and line up in single file at one end of the gym. Each team has an unbuttoned shirt on the other side of the gym. Shirts should have the same number of buttons. On the go signal, the first player in each team runs to the shirt and buttons the first button. This player then runs back to his team and tags the next player in line, who runs to the shirt and buttons the next button. The game is over when all the buttons on the shirts are buttoned. Portable sound sources should be placed by the shirts to assist children who are visually impaired, and clothing with large buttons should be used. Children who are blind should be placed with sighted partners. Aides should be available to hand shirts to children in wheelchairs.

Additional Notes: _____

_____

_____

_____

_____

_____

_____

_____

_____

_____

_____

_____

Sleeping Boogey

Equipment:	• None
Location:	• Gymnasium, outdoors
Skill Development:	Large motor, verbal communication, following directions
Abilities Required:	

Activity: One child is the "Boogey" who pretends to be asleep on one end of the gym. The other children stand at the other end of the gym. Children begin by running or skipping toward the Boogey calling, "Moonlight, Starlight, Boogey won't be out tonight!" When they get close to the boogey, she awakens and shouts, "Boo!" at which point the children turn around and run back to the other end of the gym. The Boogey gets up and chases them and the first child tagged becomes the Boogey for the next game. A portable sound source should be next to the Boogey and children should use sound-makers while running to assist children who are visually impaired. Children who are blind should be placed with sighted partners. The Boogey can tag children in wheelchairs by touching any part of their chairs.

Figure 4.13. Sleeping Boogey

Additional Notes:

Spoon and Marble Relay

Equipment:	• Spoons • Marbles
Location:	• Gymnasium, outdoors
Skill Development:	Fine motor, large motor, hand-eye coordination, visual perception, balancing
Abilities Required:	

Activity: Children line up in equal-sized teams at one end of the gym. Each child holds a spoon. The first child in each team walks to the other end of the gym and back with a marble in her spoon. She then transfers the marble from her spoon to the next player's without touching the marble. This child then walks to the end of the gym with the marble in her spoon. The game continues in this fashion until all the children have had a turn. If the marble is dropped, children must retrieve it and return it to their spoons before walking any further. Small bells can be used instead of marbles for children who are blind. A portable sound source should also be placed at the other end of the gym. Students in wheelchairs should be paired with ambulatory partners who can push their chairs.

Figure 4.14. Spoon and Marble Relay

Additional Notes:

Squirrels

Equipment:	• None
Location:	• Gymnasium, outdoors
Skill Development:	Large motor, following directions
Abilities Required:	
Activity:	Children count off in threes. Ones and twos join hands to make small circles and become "trees." Number threes stand in the middle of each circle and pretend to be "squirrels." There is one squirrel who stands alone. When the teacher gives the signal, all the squirrels run out of their trees and try to find another tree to hide in. At this point, the squirrel without a tree makes a quick dash for a tree as one of the other squirrels is leaving. When all the squirrels have found a tree, there will be one squirrel without one. The game continues in this way, but children should number off in different ways to give everyone the opportunity to be trees and squirrels. Portable sound sources should be placed near trees to assist children who are visually impaired. Children who are blind should form part of the trees or can be squirrels if paired with sighted guides. Children in wheelchairs should form trees and sit facing away from their partners to give squirrels more room.

Figure 4.15. Squirrels

Additional Notes:

Gotcha!

Equipment: • None

Location: • Gymnasium, outdoors

Skill Development: Large motor, following directions

Abilities Required:

Activity: Children are divided into two teams. Each team is given a different action that they must perform while running around the gym. Half of the children run with their hands on their heads, and the other half run with their hands on their hips. The object of the game is for members of one team to tag all members of the other team. When children are tagged they become members of the other team and continue running using the new action. The game ends when all children are on one team. Actions should be described to children who are visually impaired and students should wear sound-makers such as bells around their wrists or ankles as they are running. Children who are blind should be paired with sighted partners. Children in wheelchairs should be paired with ambulatory partners who can push their chairs while they perform the actions.

Additional Notes: _____

_____

_____

_____

_____

_____

_____

_____

_____

_____

_____

_____

Jump Up, Jump Down!

Equipment:	• None
Location:	• Gymnasium, outdoors
Skill Development:	Large motor, auditory processing, following directions, verbal communication
Abilities Required:	
Activity:	Children sit in a circle formation spaced body width apart, with one player standing in the middle. On a given signal, the children say, "Jump up, jump down, jump all around." On the word *around*, the player in the middle runs and jumps between two players in the circle. These two players get up and run around the circle in opposite directions. The last one back to her place becomes the child in the middle for the next round. Children who are blind should run with sighted partners. If the child in the middle is deaf, students should make certain hand gestures while chanting so that the child knows when to jump. If the child in the middle is in a wheelchair, the chant should be changed to, "Move left, move right, move out of sight" and the space in between children should be widened.
Additional Notes:	_____
	_____
	_____
	_____
	_____
	_____
	_____
	_____
	_____
	_____
	_____

Touch the Snake

Equipment: • Gym mats or clean floor

Location: • Gymnasium

Skill Development: Large motor, auditory processing, following directions

Abilities Required:

Activity: One child is the "starter snake" and lies down facing the floor. The other children gather around the snake and touch him with one finger. When the teacher calls, "Snake in the grass!" everybody runs to avoid being tagged by the snake. The snake slides along the floor and tries to tag as many people as possible. All those tagged become snakes and help the starter snake tag the other children. A portable sound source should be placed by the starter snake to assist children who are visually impaired, and the children should use sound-makers while running. Children who are blind should be paired with sighted partners. The teacher should wave a flag or use another signal while calling, "Snake in the grass!" for children who are deaf. If there are children in wheelchairs in the group, the starter snake should sit up to make himself easier to reach.

Figure 4.16. Touch the Snake

Additional Notes:

Weekday Race

Equipment: • None

Location: • Gymnasium, outdoors

Skill Development: Large motor, auditory processing, following directions

Abilities Required:

Activity: Children are divided into two teams and line up in horizontal lines on one side of the gym. Each player is a day of the week, with one player from each team being the same day. The teacher calls a day and the two players who are that day run to a designated point and back again. When both players are back in their original position, a different day is called. The game continues until all players have had a chance to run. This game can also be played using months, colors, or numbers. Portable sound sources should be located by the teams and at the turning point to assist children who are visually impaired. Children who are blind should run with sighted guides. The teacher should hold up signs with the words written on them for children who are deaf. Children in wheelchairs should be given the same days as each other.

Additional Notes: _____

_____

_____

_____

_____

_____

_____

_____

_____

_____

_____

_____

Zigzag Relay

Equipment:	• Pylons
Location:	• Gymnasium, outdoors
Skill Development:	Large motor, visual perception
Abilities Required:	

Activity: Children are divided into two teams and line up on one side of the gym. Pylons are arranged in zigzag formation in front of each team. On the go signal, the first player in each team runs the zigzag course and when he arrives back to the original position, he tags the hand of the next player in line who then runs the course. The game is over when all players are back in their original positions. Pylons should be striped with fluorescent tape for children who are visually impaired. Children who are blind should run with sighted guides. If there are children in wheelchairs in the group, pylons should be spread farther apart and the length of the course adapted accordingly.

Additional Notes:

_____

_____

_____

_____

_____

_____

_____

_____

_____

_____

_____

_____

_____

_____

PART THREE

Ball Games

5

Ball Games

Level 1 Activities

All ball games can be adapted in the following ways for students who are visually impaired or blind:

Beeper balls can be used. These can be purchased from companies that specialize in equipment for people with visual impairments, or may be made by cutting balls open and inserting beepers or other forms of sound-makers inside. In many activities beanbags, which can be more easily opened and resewn, can be effectively substituted for balls.

Balls that are very brightly colored or fluorescent can be used. Balls with contrasting colors, such as black on white, are also more easily visible for people with visual impairments.

Light-colored balls can be striped with black electrical tape. The contrast between the two colors makes balls easier to see.

Level 1 Ball Games

Level 1 Ball Games—by Skills

Auditory Processing

Following Directions

Visual Perception

Verbal Communication

Creative Thinking

Balancing

Air Ball

Equipment:	• Soft balls
Location:	• Gymnasium, outdoors
Skill Development:	Large motor, hand-eye coordination, visual perception
Abilities Required:	

Activity: Children stand in large circle formation, each holding a ball. On the go signal, children throw their balls into the air and attempt to catch a ball. The ball they catch can be the same ball they threw or someone else's ball. The balls that are not caught are then collected and counted. The group tries again, trying to beat their previous record. An aide or another student should be available to retrieve balls dropped by students in wheelchairs.

Figure 5.1. Air Ball

Additional Notes:

Beach Ball

Equipment: • Beach ball

Location: • Gymnasium, outdoors

Skill Development: Large motor, hand-eye coordination, visual perception

Abilities Required:

Activity: Children stand in a large circle formation. One child begins by throwing a beach ball into the air towards another child in the circle. Without catching the ball, that child hits the ball towards another child who in turn hits the ball to someone else. The game continues in this fashion with children passing the ball around the circle. The object of the game is to keep the ball airborne as long as possible. Children should count in unison as the ball is being hit so that each time the ball is dropped they can attempt to beat their record in the following round.

Figure 5.2. Beach Ball

Additional Notes:

Chase the Ball

Equipment:
- Soccer ball

Location:
- Gymnasium, outdoors

Skill Development: Large motor, hand-eye coordination, visual perception

Abilities Required:

Activity: Children are divided into groups of five or six and stand one behind the other with their legs apart. The last person in each team has a ball that she rolls forward through the other players' legs. As soon as she rolls the ball, she runs to the front of the line to try to beat the ball there. If she gets to the front of the line before the ball, she waits for the ball and then rolls it back down to the last child in line. If the ball arrives before the child, the first child in line rolls the ball back down. The game continues in this fashion until the original last child in line is back at the end of the line.

Additional Notes: _____
_____
_____
_____
_____
_____
_____
_____
_____
_____
_____
_____
_____
_____
_____
_____

Dodge the Ball

Equipment:	• Large, soft ball
Location:	• Gymnasium, outdoors
Skill Development:	Large motor, hand-eye coordination, visual perception
Abilities Required:	
Activity:	Children stand in large circle formation, about 4 feet apart. One child stands in the middle with a ball and throws it toward any child, trying to hit him below the waist. Children must dodge the ball to avoid being hit, but can only move from side to side and may not move away from the circle. Anyone who is hit by the ball leaves the circle and helps to retrieve balls that are thrown outside it. The last child left in the circle stands in the middle in the next round.
Additional Notes:	_____

_____

_____

_____

_____

_____

_____

_____

_____

_____

_____

_____

_____

_____

_____

Head Ball

Equipment:	• Large ball
Location:	• Gymnasium, outdoors
Skill Development:	Large motor, balancing
Abilities Required:	
Activity:	Children are divided into pairs. The pairs lie on their stomachs facing each other on the floor and a ball is placed between their heads. The object of the game is for the two players to try to lift the ball off of the ground while keeping it between their heads, without using their hands. The players should coordinate their movements to move from a lying to a crouching and then standing position, with the ball balanced between their heads.

Figure 5.3. Head Ball

Additional Notes:

_____

_____

_____

_____

_____

_____

_____

_____

_____

_____

_____

_____

_____

_____

_____

_____

_____

_____

_____

_____

_____

_____

_____

_____

_____

_____

_____

_____

_____

_____

_____

_____

Hoot-Chute

Equipment:	• Soft rubber ball
	• Parachute
Location:	• Gymnasium, outdoors
Skill Development:	Fine motor, large motor, auditory processing, hand-eye coordination
Abilities Required:	
Activity:	Children stand evenly spaced around a parachute, each holding on to a piece of the edge. A ball is placed on top of the parachute and the teacher gives directions as to how the parachute should be moved. Children move the parachute high and low as a group, trying not to let the ball roll over the edge. Children move their bodies up and down to get maximum movement out of the parachute. For added excitement, more balls can be added to the top of the parachute.

Figure 5.4. Hoot-Chute

Additional Notes:

Keep It Up

Equipment:	• Tennis racket or nylon stockings and wire coat hanger
	• Light ball
Location:	• Gymnasium, outdoors
Skill Development:	Fine motor, large motor, hand-eye coordination

Abilities Required:

Activity: Each child has a tennis racket or self-constructed racket made of a nylon stocking and coat hanger. Children start off individually, bouncing light balls on their rackets, trying to bounce them as many times as possible without dropping them. After children have had some time to practice, they play in doubles and then in small groups, passing the balls to one another with their rackets, attempting to keep them airborne for as long as possible. An aide should be available to pick up balls for children in wheelchairs.

Figure 5.5. Keep It Up

Additional Notes:

Kick the Ball

Equipment:	• Soft ball
Location:	• Gymnasium, outdoors
Skill Development:	Large motor, visual perception
Abilities Required:	
Iactivity:	Children stand in circle formation with hands joined. One child stands in the middle and kicks a ball to a child in the circle, who in turn kicks it to someone else. The ball continues to be gently kicked around the circle. The child in the middle must remain stationary and can move his legs only to kick the ball. If the ball passes him, he tries to kick it out of the circle. Children try to stop the ball from going in between their legs or the space to their right. If the ball passes through either of these spaces, the player who let it through changes places with the child in the middle.
Additional Notes:	

Flying Ball

Equipment:	• Large ball
Location:	• Gymnasium, outdoors
Skill Development:	Large motor, auditory processing, hand-eye coordination, visual perception, verbal communication

Abilities Required:

Activity: Children stand in circle formation. One child stands in the middle and throws a ball in the air while calling someone's name. The child whose name is called tries to catch the ball before it touches the ground. If he catches the ball, he trades places with the child in the middle and throws the ball for another child to catch. If he does not catch the ball, the child in the middle continues to call names and throw the ball until a child succeeds in catching it before it bounces. If there are students who are deaf in the group, children should stand spaced farther apart and the child in the middle should directly face them while throwing the ball.

Additional Notes: _____

_____

_____

_____

_____

_____

_____

_____

_____

_____

_____

_____

_____

Music Ball

Equipment:	• Music source • Soft ball
Location:	• Gymnasium
Skill Development:	Large motor, hand-eye coordination, following directions, creative thinking
Abilities Required:	

Activity: Children stand in circle formation. Music is played and the ball is passed around the circle until the music stops, at which point the child with the ball thinks of a different way to pass it on to the next person, such as under a leg, or rolled down an arm. Children then pass the ball around the circle using this new motion. Every time the music stops, the child with the ball thinks of a different way of passing it on. Verbal directions should be given to children who are blind. A flag should be waved or another signal used to indicate that the music has stopped for children who are deaf.

Additional Notes: _____

_____

_____

_____

_____

_____

_____

_____

_____

_____

_____

_____

_____

Over and Over

Equipment: • Ball

Location: • Gymnasium, outdoors

Skill Development: Large motor, hand-eye coordination, visual perception

Abilities Required:

Activity: Children line up one behind the other, standing about 1 foot apart. The
                      first child in line has a ball that she passes backward over her head to the
                      child behind. As soon as the child receives the ball, the child who passed
                      it runs to the end of the line. The game continues in this way with chil-
                      dren passing the ball behind them and running to the end of the line. The
                      game ends when the original first child in line is back at the front of the
                      line. A portable sound source should be placed at the end of the line to as-
                      sist children who are visually impaired.

Figure 5.6. Over and Over

Additional Notes:

Pass the Ball

Equipment:	• Soccer ball
Location:	• Gymnasium, outdoors
Skill Development:	Large motor, hand-eye coordination, visual perception
Abilities Required:	 
Activity:	Children are divided into groups of three. Two players run across the gym about 20 feet apart, passing a ball back and forth as they go. The third player stands in between them and tries to intercept a pass. If he is successful, the player who passed the ball takes on the role of the interceptor and the interceptor takes his place. The game continues in this fashion with children passing the ball to their partners while running up and down the gym.

Figure 5.7. Pass the Ball

Additional Notes:

Square Ball

Equipment: • Large ball

                      • Chalk or tape

Location: • Gymnasium, outdoors

Skill Development: Large motor, hand-eye coordination, visual perception

Abilities Required:

Activity: Large squares are marked on the ground with masking tape; they are arranged in groups of four. One child stands in each square. The game begins with one child bouncing a ball to a player in another square. That child hits the ball to someone in another square. That player, in turn, bounces the ball to another child. Children must stay within the squares while hitting the ball to one another. Squares should be big enough to accommodate children in wheelchairs. If there are students who are blind in the group, children should say their names out loud while bouncing the balls to them. Students should use sound-makers to assist children who are blind to return the ball.

Figure 5.8. Square Ball

Additional Notes:

Towel Toss

Equipment:	• Large ball
	• Beach towels
Location:	• Gymnasium, outdoors
Skill Development:	Fine motor, large motor, hand-eye coordination, visual perception
Abilities Required:	

Activity: Children are divided into pairs, each with a large towel and a ball. Each player holds on to one end of the outstretched towel, and the ball is placed in the middle. The object of the game is for the children to toss the ball into the air and catch it on the towel. Children count to see how many times they can toss the ball without it falling on the floor and should try to beat their record each time. As students get better, they should try to throw the ball higher.

Figure 5.9. Towel Toss

Additional Notes:

Wall Bounce

Equipment: • Tennis balls

Location: • Gymnasium, outdoors

Skill Development: Large motor, hand-eye coordination, visual perception

Abilities Required:

Activity: Children are divided into groups of five or six. Each group stands in a horizontal line, facing a wall. The first child throws a ball at the wall so the next child can catch it, either on a bounce or on the fly. When the second child catches it, she bounces it off the wall for the next child to catch. This process is repeated all the way down the line until the last child has the ball. The game then continues in the other direction as the last player bounces the ball back to the child he just received it from. An aide should be available to pick up balls dropped by children in wheelchairs.

Figure 5.10. Wall Bounce

Additional Notes:

Stop the Ball

Equipment:	• Ball
Location:	• Gymnasium, outdoors
Skill Development:	Large motor, hand-eye coordination, visual perception

Abilities Required:

Activity: Children stand in circle formation with their feet spread comfortably apart. Each child's right foot touches the next player's left foot. One child stands in the middle and tries to roll or kick the ball out of the circle through a space between the children's legs. The circled players try to stop the ball from getting through with their hands, without moving the position of their feet. Any player who lets the ball pass through her legs changes place with the child in the middle. Children who are blind should stand next to sighted children.

Additional Notes: _____

_____

_____

_____

_____

_____

_____

_____

_____

_____

_____

_____

_____

_____

_____

6

Ball Games

Level 2 Activities

Level 2 Ball Games

Level 2 Ball Games—by Skills

Animal Catch

Equipment:	• Soft ball
Location:	• Gymnasium, outdoors
Skill Development:	Large motor, hand-eye coordination, visual perception
Abilities Required:	

Activity: Children stand in circle formation, and each child calls out the name of a different animal. One child stands in the middle with a ball and calls out, "The ball goes to the cat," while throwing the ball to the child who is the "cat." If this child does not catch the ball, the children exchange places and the cat throws the ball to another child in the circle. If she does catch the ball, she throws it back to the child in the middle who then chooses a new animal to throw it to. The game continues in this fashion, with the child in the middle throwing the ball to different animals around the circle.

Additional Notes: _____

_____

_____

_____

_____

_____

_____

_____

_____

_____

_____

_____

_____

_____

_____

_____

Beat the Ball

Equipment: • Large balls

Location: • Gymnasium, outdoors

Skill Development: Large motor, hand-eye coordination, visual perception

Abilities Required:

Activity: Children stand in pairs at one end of the gym, all facing the same direction. One child in each pair rolls a ball as hard as she can toward the opposite end of the gym. As soon as the ball hits the ground, both children run to the other end and try to "beat the ball." When the children reach the other end, they retrieve the ball and line up facing the other end of the gym. This time the other child in the pair rolls the ball.

Additional Notes: _____

_____

_____

_____

_____

_____

_____

_____

_____

_____

_____

_____

_____

_____

_____

_____

Guard Me

Equipment:	• Soft ball
	• Chair
Location:	• Gymnasium, outdoors
Skill Development:	Large motor, hand-eye coordination, visual perception
Abilities Required:	

Activity: Children stand in large circle formation. One child sits on a chair inside the circle, while another child stands in front of him, acting as the "guard." Children take turns tossing a ball and trying to hit the seated child below the waist. The guard tries to keep him from being hit by blocking the ball, then returning it to someone else in the circle. Children in the circle may also pass the ball to other players who may be in a better position to hit the child. When a child is successful, she exchanges places with the guard and another child is chosen to sit in the middle. A portable sound source should be placed in front of the chair to assist children who are blind.

Figure 6.1. Guard Me

Additional Notes:

Catch the Ball

Equipment:	• Soft ball
Location:	• Gymnasium, outdoors
Skill Development:	Large motor, hand-eye coordination, visual perception
Abilities Required:	

Activity: Children run freely around the gym. One child has a ball and begins the game by calling "Stop!" at which point all the players stop in their tracks. The child with the ball takes three steps towards any player and attempts to hit him with the ball below the waist. The targeted player must keep her feet fixed on the ground. If she is hit she must run and retrieve the ball while the other children continue running around the gym. When she has the ball in her possession, she calls out "Stop!" and attempts to hit another child. If she misses, she must again retrieve the ball, while the other children continue running. Children who are blind should be paired with sighted partners. Children who are non-verbal should blow a whistle as the "Stop!" command. If there are children in wheelchairs, the child with the ball can hit any part of their chairs. An aide should be available to hand the ball to children in wheelchairs after they have been hit.

Additional Notes: _____

_____

_____

_____

_____

_____

_____

_____

_____

_____

_____

_____

H·O·R·S·E

Equipment:

- Basketball
- Basketball basket

Location:

- Gymnasium, outdoors

Skill Development:

Large motor, hand-eye coordination, visual perception

Abilities Required:

Activity:

Children stand in line and take turns shooting a ball into a basketball net from anywhere on the court. When a basket is made, the next player in line makes the shot from the same position on the court as the player who made the basket. If he misses, he calls out, "H!" and goes to the end of the line. The next child can then shoot from anywhere on the court. If he makes the basket, the following player must make the shot from the same position. If she misses, she too calls out "H." The next time they miss, they call out "O." The game continues in this way until someone becomes H-O-R-S-E. A beeper should be attached to the basket to assist children who are visually impaired.

Figure 6.2. H-O-R-S-E

Additional Notes:

Keep Away!

Equipment:	• Ball • Arm bands
Location:	• Gymnasium, outdoors
Skill Development:	Large motor, hand-eye coordination, visual perception, verbal communication
Abilities Required:	
Activity:	Children are divided into two teams. One team passes a ball among themselves while the other team attempts to intercept a pass. The passing team should wear arm bands to be identified to team members. The object of the game is for the team to pass the ball five consecutive times without having it intercepted by the other team. As the ball is passed, all members of the passing team call out the number of the pass. Once the ball is intercepted, the count goes back to "one." Each time a team completes five consecutive passes, the ball is given to the opposing team and the same procedure is followed. If all children in the group are nonverbal, the teacher should call out the number of the pass.
Additional Notes:	_____ _____ _____ _____ _____ _____ _____ _____ _____ _____ _____

Name Ball

Equipment:	• Soft ball
	• Net
Location:	• Gymnasium, outdoors
Skill Development:	Large motor, hand-eye coordination, visual perception
Abilities Required:	

Activity: Children are divided into two equal-sized groups and stand on either side of a net. One child begins the game by calling out a child's name on the other team and throwing a ball to her. The child whose name is called should try to catch the ball, but her team mates can help out if the ball is closer to them. If no one catches the ball, the child whose name was called moves to the other side of the net and joins the other team. The game ends when all the children are on the same team. If children are non-verbal or deaf, the ball should be thrown to the child standing directly opposite on the other side of the net.

Figure 6.3. Name Ball

Additional Notes:

_____

_____

_____

_____

_____

_____

_____

_____

_____

_____

_____

_____

_____

_____

_____

_____

_____

_____

_____

_____

_____

_____

_____

_____

_____

_____

_____

_____

Pirates

Equipment: • Soft balls

Location: • Gymnasium, outdoors

Skill Development: Large motor, hand-eye coordination, visual perception

Abilities Required:

Activity: Children are divided into two groups, one larger than the other. Each child in the larger group is given a ball to bounce or dribble around the gym. The other children are "pirates" who try to take the balls away from the children without making any body contact. The children with the balls try to stop their balls from being taken by dodging the pirates and running away while bouncing or dribbling their balls. When a pirate succeeds in taking a ball, the children change roles and the child who lost her ball becomes a pirate and in turn tries to take another player's ball.

Additional Notes: _____

_____

_____

_____

_____

_____

_____

_____

_____

_____

_____

_____

_____

_____

_____

Soccer Baseball

Equipment:	• Soccer ball
	• Pylons
Location:	• Gymnasium, outdoors
Skill Development:	Large motor, following directions, visual perception

Abilities Required:

Activity: This game is similar to baseball, except the ball is kicked rather than batted. Children are divided into two teams, one being the kicking team and the other being the fielders. Four pylons are laid out in a circle, acting as three bases and a home plate. One child is the "pitcher," who rolls the ball on the floor to the first player in his team. This player kicks the ball and runs to the first pylon. In order for fielders to get the player out, they must catch the ball and roll it at the player, hitting him before he reaches the pylon. When one team is out, the roles are reversed and the previous kickers become the fielders. Portable sound sources should be placed next to the pylons to assist children who are visually impaired. Children in wheelchairs should throw balls and are out when any parts of their chairs are hit with balls by the fielders.

Additional Notes:

Under the Tunnel, Over the Bridge

Equipment: • Large ball

Location: • Gymnasium, outdoors

Skill Development: Large motor, hand-eye coordination, visual perception

Abilities Required:

Activity: Children stand in a line, one behind the other, an arm's length apart. The first child passes a ball to the player behind by passing it over his head. The second player passes the ball to the child behind her by placing it between her legs, and the third child passes it over her head. This pattern continues down the line with children passing the ball over their heads and between their legs. When the ball reaches the last child, she runs with the ball to the front of the line and starts the process over. The game ends when the original first player is back at the front of the line. Children in wheelchairs should pass balls over their heads. When a child in a wheelchair is moving to the front of the line, an aide should be available to hold the ball for her or to push the chair to the front of the line while the child holds the ball.

Figure 6.4. Under the Tunnel, Over the Bridge

Additional Notes:

CORWIN PRESS

The Corwin Press logo—a raven striding across an open book—represents the happy union of courage and learning. We are a professional-level publisher of books and journals for K-12 educators, and we are committed to creating and providing resources that embody these qualities. Corwin's motto is "Success for All Learners."